Presented To

_____

On the occasion of

_____

From

_____

Date

_____

The GREATEST

Thing in the

World

In Today's Language

© 1994 by Barbour and Company, Inc.

ISBN 1-55748-547-X

 Member of the
Evangelical Christian
Publishers Association

Published by Barbour and Company, Inc.
            P.O. Box 719
            Uhrichsville, Ohio 44683

Printed in the United States of America

HENRY DRUMMOND

THE GREATEST THING IN THE WORLD

IN TODAY'S LANGUAGE

L • O • V • E

Edited by Carolyn Linn

A Barbour Book

The first time the noted evangelist Dwight L. Moody heard Henry Drummond deliver this meditation on the thirteenth chapter of 1 Corinthians he said he had never heard anything so beautiful. "The one great need in our Christian life is love, more love to God and to each other," he later wrote. "Would that we could all move into that Love chapter, and live there."

Henry Drummond himself never dreamed his words would have any lasting value, but *The Greatest Thing in the World* endures today and is his legacy. Indeed, the need for genuine Christian love remains as great as ever. Of faith, hope, and love, love is "the greatest of these" because it alone is the fulfilling of all of God's laws.

This beloved classic, which teaches the art of living and loving abundantly, as Christ intended, will inspire you to share God's love through unselfish acts of kindness. Begin today to bring yourself and those around you closer to God.

*I*f I speak in the tongues of men and of angels, but have not love, I am only a resounding gong or a clanging cymbal. If I have the gift of prophecy and can fathom all mysteries and all knowledge, and if I have a faith that can move mountains, but have no love, I am nothing. If I give all I possess to the poor and surrender my body to the flames, but have not love, I gain nothing.

Love is patient, love is kind. It does not envy, it does not boast, it is not proud. It is not rude, it is not self-seeking, it is not easily angered, it keeps no record of wrongs. Love does not delight in evil but rejoices with the truth. It always protects, always trusts, always hopes, always perseveres.

Love never fails. But where there are prophecies, they will cease; where there are tongues, they will be stilled; where there is knowledge, it will pass away. For we know in part and we prophesy in part, but when perfection comes, the imperfect disappears. When I was a child, I talked like a child, I thought like a child, I reasoned like a child. When I became a man, I put childish ways behind me. Now we see but a poor reflection as a mirror; then we shall see face to face. Now I know in part; then I shall know fully, even as I am fully known.

And now these three remain: faith, hope and love. But the greatest of these is love.

1 Corinthians 13
New International Version

THE *GREATEST THING* IN THE *WORLD*

Since ancient times, people have asked themselves this question: What is the greatest thing in the world? You have life before you. You can only live it once. What is the noblest object of desire, the supreme gift to covet?

We are used to being told that the greatest thing in the religious world is faith. For centuries that great word has been Christianity's keynote, and we have easily learned to look on it as the greatest thing in the world. Well, we are wrong. If we have been told that, we may miss the mark. I have taken you, in the chapter that I have just read, to Christianity at its source; and there we have seen, "The greatest of these is love." It is not an oversight. Paul was speaking of faith just a moment before. He says, "If I have all faith, so that I can remove mountains, and have not love, I am nothing." So far from forgetting, he deliberately contrasts them, "Now abideth faith, hope, love," and without a moment's hesitation, the decision falls, "The greatest of these is love."

And it is not prejudice. People are apt to recommend to others their own strong points. The observing student can detect a beautiful tenderness growing and ripening all through his character as Paul gets old; but the hand that wrote, "The greatest of these is love," when we meet it first, is stained with blood.

Nor is this letter to the Corinthians peculiar in singling out love as the greatest good. The masterpieces of Christianity are agreed about it. Peter says, "Above all things have fervent love among yourselves." *Above all things.* And John goes further: "God is love." Remember the profound remark that Paul makes elsewhere: "Love is the fulfilling of the law." Did you ever think what he meant by that?

In those days people were working their passage to heaven by keeping the Ten Commandments, and the hundred and ten things, without ever thinking about them. If you love, you will unconsciously fulfill the whole law. And you can readily see for yourselves how that must be so. Take any of the commandments. "Thou shalt have no other gods before Me." If a person loves God, you will not need to tell him that. Love is the fulfilling of that law. "Take not His name in vain." Would someone who loves God ever dream of taking His name in vain? "Remember the Sabbath day to keep it holy." Those who truly love God are only too glad to have one day in seven to dedicate more exclusively to Him. Love would fulfill all these laws regarding God. Similarly, if someone loved his neighbor, you would never think of telling him to honor his father and mother. He could not do anything else. It would be preposterous to tell him not to kill. You could only insult him if you suggested that he should not steal—how could he steal from those he loved? It would be superfluous to beg him not to bear false witness against his neighbor. If he loved him it would be the last thing he would do. And you would never dream of urging him not to covet what his neighbors had. He would rather they possessed it than himself. In this way, "Love is the fulfilling of the law."

It is the rule for fulfilling all rules, the new commandment for keeping all the old commandments, Christ's one secret of the Christian life.

Paul had learned this truth; in this noble eulogy he has given us the most wonderful and original account of this greatest gift. We can divide it into three parts: In the beginning of the short chapter, we have love contrasted; in the heart of it, we have love analyzed; toward the end we have love defended as the supreme gift.

THE CONTRAST

Paul begins by contrasting love with other things that men in those days esteemed. I won't attempt to go over those things in detail. Their inferiority is already obvious.

Then he contrasts love with eloquence. And what a noble gift it is, the power of playing upon the souls and wills of men and women and rousing them to lofty purposes and holy deeds. Yet Paul says, "If I speak with the tongues of men and of angels, and have not love, I am becoming as sounding brass, or a tinkling cymbal." And we all know why. We have all felt the brazenness of words without emotion, the hollowness, the unaccountable unpersuasiveness, of eloquence behind which lies no love.

He contrasts it with prophecy. He contrasts it with mysteries. He contrasts it with faith. He contrasts it with charity. Why is love greater than faith? Because the end is greater than the means. And why is it greater than charity? Because the whole is greater than the part. Love is greater than faith, because the end is greater than the means. What is the use of having faith? It is to connect the soul with God. And what is the object of connecting one's soul with God? To become like God. But God is love. Hence faith, the means, exists in order to love, the end. Love, therefore, obviously is greater than faith. It is greater than charity, again, because the whole is greater than a part. Charity is only a little bit of love, one of the innumerable avenues of love, and there may even be, and there is, a great deal of charity without love. It is an easy thing to toss a coin to a beggar in the street; it is generally an easier thing to do it than not. Yet love is just as often in the withholding. We purchase relief from the sympathetic feelings aroused by the spectacle of misery, at the cost of a penny. It is too cheap—too cheap for us, and often too dear for the beggar. If we really loved him we would either do more for him, or less.

Then Paul contrasts it with sacrifice and martyrdom. And I beg the little band of would-be missionaries—and I have the honor to call some of you by this name for the first time—to remember that though you give your bodies to be burned, and have not love, it profits nothing—nothing! You can take nothing greater to the unchurched world than the mark and reflection of the love of God on your own character. That is the universal language. It will take you years to speak Chinese, or the dialects of India. From the day you land, however, that language of love, understood by all, will be pouring forth its unconscious eloquence. It is the man or woman who is the missionary, it is not his or her words. Character is the message. In the heart of Africa, among the great Lakes, I have come across men and women who remembered the only white man they ever saw before—David Livingstone; and as you cross his footsteps in that continent, men's faces will light up as they speak of the kind doctor who passed there years ago. They could not understand him; but they felt the love that beat in his heart. Take into your new sphere of labor, where you also mean to lay down your life, that simple charm, and your life work must succeed. You can take nothing greater, you need take nothing less. It is not worthwhile going if you take anything less. You may take every accomplishment; you may be braced for every sacrifice; but if you give your body to be burned, and have not love, it will profit you and the cause of Christ nothing.

THE *A*NALYSIS

*A*fter contrasting love with these other, less important, things, Paul gives us in three short verses an amazing analysis of this supreme thing. It is a compound thing, he tells us. It is life light. As you have seen a scientist take a beam of light and pass it through a crystal prism, as you have seen it come out on the other side of the prism broken up unto its component colors—red, blue, yellow, violet, orange, and all the colors of the rainbow—so Paul passes this thing, love, through the magnificent prism of his inspired intellect, and it comes out on the other side broken up into its elements. And in these few words we have what one might call the spectrum of love, the analysis of love. Notice that they have common names; they are virtues that we hear about every day; they are things that can be practiced by every person in every walk of life. Thus, the supreme thing is made up of a multitude of small things and ordinary virtues.

The spectrum of love has nine ingredients:

Patience—"Love suffereth long."
Kindness—"And is kind."
Generosity—"Love envieth not."
Humility—"Love vaunteth not itself, is not puffed up."

Courtesy—"Doth not behave itself unseemly."
Unselfishness—"Seeketh not her own."
Good temper—"Is not easily provoked."
Guilelessness—"Thinketh no evil."
Sincerity—"Rejoiceth not in iniquity,
but rejoiceth in the truth."

Patience; kindness; generosity; humility; courtesy; unselfishness; good temper; guilelessness; sincerity— these make up the supreme gift, the stature of the perfect person.

All these qualities are in relation to people, in relation to life, in relation to the known today and the near tomorrow, and not to the unknown eternity. We hear much of love to God; Christ spoke much of people loving each other. We make a great deal of peace

THE GREATEST THING IN THE WORLD

with heaven; Christ made much of peace on earth.
Religion is not a strange or added thing, but the
inspiration of the secular life, the breathing of an
eternal spirit through this temporal world. The
supreme thing, in short, is not a thing at all, but the
giving of a further finish to the multitudinous words
and acts that make up the sum of every common day.

There is not time to do more than make a pass-
ing comment about each of these ingredients.

Patience. This is the normal attitude of love; love
passive, love waiting to begin; not in a hurry; calm;
ready to do its work when the summons comes but
meantime wearing the ornament of a meek and quiet
spirit. Love suffers long; beareth all things; believeth
all things; hopeth all things. For love understands,
and therefore waits.

Kindness. Love active. Have you every noticed

— 24 —

how much of Christ's life was spent doing kind
things—in merely doing kind things? Think about
His life with that in mind, and you will realize that
He spent a great proportion of His time simply
making people happy, doing good deeds for people.
There is only one thing greater than happiness in
the world, and that is holiness; we have no power to
create holiness in people, but what God has put in
our power is the ability to influence those around us
to be happy—something we manage largely by being
kind to them.

"The greatest thing a man can do for his Heavenly
Father," someone once said, "is to be kind to some of
His other children." I wonder why it is that we are not
all kinder than we are. How much the world needs it.
How easily it is done. How instantaneously it acts.
How infallibly it is remembered. How superabundant-

ly it pays itself back—for there is no debtor in the world so honorable as love. "Love never faileth." Love is success, love is happiness, love is life. "Love," I say with Browning, "is the energy of Life."

> "For life, with all it yields of joy and woe
>   And hope and fear,
>   Is just our chance o' the prize of learning
>   love—
>   How love might be, hath been indeed,
>   and is."

Where love is, God is. He that dwelleth in love dwelleth in God. God is love. Therefore love. Without distinction, without calculation, without procrastination, love. Lavish it on the poor, where it is easy; especially on the rich, who often need it most; most of all on your friends, where it is difficult, and for whom perhaps we each do least of all. There is a difference between trying to please and giving pleasure. Give pleasure. Lose no chance of giving pleasure. For that is the ceaseless and anonymous triumph of a truly loving spirit. "I will pass through this world but once. Any good thing therefore that I can do, or any kindness that I can show to any human being, let me do it now. Let me not defer it or neglect it, for I shall not pass this way again."

Generosity. "Love envieth not." This is love in competition with others. Whenever you attempt a good work, you will find others doing the same kind of work, and probably doing it better. Do not envy them. Envy is a feeling of ill will toward those who are in the same line as ourselves, a spirit of covetousness and detraction. Even doing Christian work is little protection against harboring this most un-Christian feeling. That most despicable of all the unworthy moods that cloud a Christian's soul assuredly waits for us on the threshold of every work, unless we are fortified with this grace of magnanimity. The Christian only truly needs to envy one thing: the large, rich, generous soul that "envieth not."

Humility. After having learned all that, you have to learn one thing more: to put a seal upon your lips and forget what you have done. After you have been kind, after love has done its beautiful work, go back into the shade again and say nothing about it. Love hides even from itself. Love waives even self-satisfaction. "Love vaunteth not itself, is not puffed up."

Courtesy. The fifth ingredient is a somewhat strange one to find. This is love in society, love in relation to etiquette. "Love doth not behave itself

unseemly." Politeness has been defined as love in tri-
fles. Courtesy is said to be love in little things. The
one secret of politeness is to love. Love cannot
behave itself unseemly. You can put the most untu-
tored person into the highest society, and if she has a
reservoir of love in her heart, she will not behave
unseemly. She simply cannot do it. Carlyle said there
was no truer gentleman in Europe than Robert
Burns, the ploughman poet. It was because he loved
everything—the mouse, and the daisy, and all the
things, great and small, that God had made. So with
this simple passport he could mingle with any society,
and enter courts and palaces from his little cottage
on the banks of the Ayr. A "gentleman" is a gentle
man—a man who does things gently, with love. And
that is the whole art and mystery of it. The gentle
man cannot do an ungentle, an ungentlemanly thing.

— 29 —

The ungentle soul, the inconsiderate, unsympathetic nature cannot do anything else. "Love doth not behave itself unseemly."

Unselfishness. "Love seeketh not her own." Observe: seeketh not even that which is her own. In Great Britain the average citizen is devoted, and rightly, to his or her rights. But there come times when a person may exercise the even higher right of giving up his or her rights. Yet Paul does not summon us to give up our rights. Love strikes much deeper. It would have us not seek them at all, ignore them, eliminate the personal element altogether from our calculations. It is not hard to give up our rights. They are often external. More difficult is not to seek things for ourselves at all. After we have sought them, bought them, won them, deserved them, we have taken the cream off them for ourselves already. It's a small sacrifice, then, perhaps, to give them up. But not to seek them at all—that is a much deeper and more difficult sacrifice. "Seekest thou great things for thyself?" said the prophet. "Seek them not." Why? Because there is no greatness in things. Things cannot be great. The only greatness is unselfish love. Even self-denial in itself is nothing, is almost a mistake. Only a great purpose or a mightier love can justify the waste. It is more difficult, I have said, not to seek our own at all, than, having sought it, to give it up. I must take that back. It is only true of a partly selfish heart. Nothing is a hardship to love, and nothing is hard. I believe that Christ's yoke is easy. Christ's "yoke" is just His way of taking life. And I believe it is an easier way than any other. I believe it is a happier way than any other. The most obvious lesson in Christ's teaching is that there is no happiness in having and getting anything, but only in giving. (I repeat there is no happiness in having, or in getting, but only in giving.) Unfortunately, half the world is on the wrong scent in the pursuit of happiness. They think it comes from having and getting, and in being served by others instead of giving and serving. He that would be great among you, said Christ, let him serve. He that would be happy, let him remember that there is but one way—it is more blessed, it is more happy, to give than to receive.

Good temper. The next ingredient is a remarkable one. "Love is not easily provoked." Nothing could be more striking than to find this here. We are inclined to look on bad temper as a harmless weakness. We speak of it as a mere infirmity of nature, a family failing, a matter of temperament, not a thing to take into serious account in estimating a person's character. And yet here, right in the heart of this analysis of love, it finds a place; and the Bible again and again returns to condemn it as one of the most destructive elements in human nature.

The peculiarity of ill temper is that it is the vice of the virtuous. It is often the one blot on an otherwise noble character. You know men and women who are all but perfect but for an easily ruffled, quick-tempered, or "touchy" disposition. This compatibility of ill temper with high moral character is one of the strangest and saddest problems of ethics. The truth is there are two great classes of sins—sins of the body and sins of the disposition. The prodigal son is a type of the first, his elder brother of the second. Now society has no doubt whatever which of these is the worse: the prodigal. But are we right? We have no balance to weigh one another's sins, and coarser and finer are but human words; but faults in the higher nature may be less pardonable than those in the lower, and to the eye of Him who is love, a sin against love may seem a hundred times more base. No form of vice—not worldliness, not greed, not drunkenness—does more to un-Christianize society than evil temper. For embittering life, for breaking up communities, for destroying the most sacred relationships, for devastating homes, for withering up men and women, for taking the bloom off childhood; in short, for sheer gratuitous misery-producing power, this influence stands alone. Look at the elder brother, moral, hard-working, patient, dutiful—let him get all credit for his virtues—look at this man, this baby, sulking outside his own father's door. "He was angry," we read, "and would not go in." Consider his behavior's effect on the father, on the servants, on the happiness of the guests. Judge the effect upon the prodigal. How many prodigals are kept out of the kingdom of God by the unlovely characters of those who profess to be inside? Analyze, as a study in temper, the thundercloud itself as it gathers on the elder brother's face. What is it made of? Jealousy, anger, pride, cruelty, self-right-eousness, touchiness, doggedness, sullenness—these are the ingredients of this dark and loveless soul. In varying proportions, also, these are the ingredients of all ill temper. Aren't sins of the disposition worse to live in, and for others to live with, than sins of the body? Christ answered the question Himself when He said, "I say unto you, that the publicans and the har-lots go into the kingdom of heaven before you." There is really no place in heaven for a disposition like this. Someone with such a mood could only make heaven miserable for all the people in it. Unless, therefore, such a man be born again, he cannot, he simply cannot, enter the kingdom of heaven. For it is perfectly certain—and you will not misunderstand me— that those who wish to enter heaven must take heaven with them.

You will see, then, that temper is significant not only for what it is, but for what it reveals. This is why I take the liberty of speaking of it with such unusual plainness. It is a symptom, a revelation of a nature that is, at bottom, unloving. It is the intermittent fever that signals unremitting disease within; the occasional bubble escaping to the surface that betrays some rottenness underneath; a sample of the most hidden products of the soul dropped involuntarily when off one's guard; in a word, the lightning form of a hundred hideous and un-Christian sins. A lack of patience, a lack of kindness, a lack of generosity, a lack of courtesy, a lack of unselfishness, are all instantaneously symbolized in one flash of temper.

It is not enough, therefore, to deal with the temper. We must go to the source and change the inmost nature so the ill temper will die away by itself. Souls are made sweet not by taking the acid fluids out, but by putting something in—a great love, a new spirit, the Spirit of Christ. When Christ's Spirit penetrates ours, it sweetens, purifies, and transforms. Only this can eradicate what is wrong, work a chemical change, renovate and regenerate, and rehabilitate the inner person. Neither willpower nor time changes men and women. Christ does. Therefore, "Let that mind be in you which was also in Christ Jesus." Some of us don't have much time to lose. This is a matter of life or death. I cannot help speaking urgently, for myself, for yourselves. "Whoso shall offend one of these little ones, which believe in me, it were better for him that a millstone were hanged about his neck, and that he were drowned in the depth of the sea." That is to say, it is the deliberate verdict of the Lord Jesus that it is better not to live than not to love. *It is better not to live than not to love.*

Guilelessness and *sincerity*. These may be dismissed almost with a word. Guilelessness is the grace for suspicious people, and the possession of it is the great secret of personal influence. You will find, if you think for a moment, that the people who influence you are people who believe in you. In an atmosphere of suspicion you shrivel up; but in an atmosphere of acceptance you expand and find encouragement and educative fellowship. It is a wonderful thing that here and there in this hard, uncharitable world there are still a few rare souls who think no evil. This is the great unworldliness. Love "thinketh no evil," imputes no motive, sees the bright side, puts the best construction on every action. What a delightful state of mind! What a stimulus and blessing to meet such a friend for a day! To be trusted is to be saved. And if we try to influence or elevate others, we will soon see that success is in proportion to their belief that we believe in them. When a person has the respect of another, his or her self-respect begins to grow and he or she can realize their full potential.

Sincerity. The Authorized Version says, "Love rejoiceth not in iniquity, but rejoiceth in the truth." I have called the quality described in this verse sincerity. The person who loves will love truth wholeheartedly. They will rejoice in the truth—not in what they have been taught to believe, not in this Church's doctrine or in that, not in this ism or in that ism, but "in the truth." They will accept only what is real and will strive to get the facts; they will search for truth with a humble and unbiased mind and cherish whatever they find at any sacrifice. But the Revised Version's more literal translation calls for just such a sacrifice for truth's sake here. This version says, "Rejoiceth not in unrighteousness, but rejoiceth with the truth," a quality that probably no one English word—and certainly not sincerity—adequately defines. It includes, perhaps more strictly, the self-restraint that refuses to gain from others' faults; the charity that doesn't delight in exposing the weakness of others, but "covereth all things"; the sincerity of purpose that endeavors to see things as they are, and rejoices to find them better than suspicion feared or rumors denounced.

So much for the analysis of love. The real business of our lives is to have these things molded into our characters. That is the supreme work we need to strive to accomplish in this world: to learn love. Life is full of opportunities for learning love. Every man and woman, every day, has a thousand of them. The world is not a playground; it is a classroom. Life is not a holiday, but an education, and the one eternal lesson for us all is how to love better.

What makes someone a good ballplayer? Practice. What makes someone a good artist, a good sculptor, a good musician? Practice. What makes someone a good teacher, a good secretary? Practice. What makes someone a good person? Practice. Nothing else. There is nothing capricious about religion. We do not develop the soul in different ways, under different laws, from those in which we develop the body and the mind. If you don't exercise your arm, you won't develop your biceps; and if you don't exercise your soul, you won't develop strength of character, vigor of moral fiber, or beauty of spiritual growth. Love is not a thing of enthusiastic emotion. It is a rich, vigorous expression of the whole Christian character—the Christlike nature in its fullest development. And the constituents of this great character can only be built up by ceaseless practice.

What was Christ doing in the carpenter's shop? Practicing. Though perfect, we read that He learned obedience. He increased in wisdom and in favor with God and man. Therefore, don't complain about your lot in life and its never-ceasing cares, its petty environment, the vexations you have to stand, the small and sordid individuals you have to live and work with. Above all, don't resent temptation; don't be perplexed because it seems to thicken around you more and more, seemingly unaffected by effort, agony, or prayer. These things are the practice that God has given you, and they are your opportunities to grow patient, humble, generous, unselfish, kind, and courteous. Do not grudge the hand that is molding the still too shapeless image within you. Even though you can't see it, it is growing steadily more beautiful, and every touch of temptation may add to its perfection. Do not isolate yourself. Be among people and among things, and among troubles, difficulties, and obstacles. Remember Goethe's words: Es bildet ein Talent sich in der Stille, Doch ein Character in dem Strom der Welt. "Talent develops itself in solitude; character in the stream of life." Talent develops itself in solitude—the talent of prayer, of faith, of mediation, of seeing the unseen. Character grows in the stream of the world's life. That chiefly is where we are to learn love.

THE GREATEST THING IN THE WORLD

How? Now, how? To make it easier, I have named a few of the elements of love. But these are only elements. Love itself can never be defined. As light is something more than the sum of its ingredients, so love is something more than a palpitating, quivering, sensitive, living thing. By synthesis of all the colors we can make whiteness, but we cannot make light. By synthesis of all the virtues, we can create love. How then are we to have this transcendent living whole conveyed into our souls? We attempt to secure it. We try to copy those who have it. We lay down rules about it. We watch. We pray. But these things alone will not bring love into our nature. Love is an effect. And only as we fulfill the right condition can we have the effect produced. Shall I tell you the cause?

If you turn to the Revised Version of the First Epistle of John, you will find these words: "We love,

— 44 —

because He first loved us." "We love," not "We love Him." That is the way the old version has it, and it is quite wrong. "We love—because He first loved us." Look at that word "because." It is the cause of which I have spoken. "Because He first loved us," the effect follows that we love: We love Him, we love all people. We cannot help it. Our hearts are slowly changed. Contemplate the love of Christ, and you will love. Stand before that mirror, reflect Christ's character, and you will be changed into the same image from tenderness to tenderness. There is no other way. You cannot love to order. You can only look at the lovely object, fall in love with it, and grow into its likeness. And so look at this Perfect Character, this Perfect Life. Look at the great sacrifice as He laid down Himself, all through life, and on the Cross of Calvary; and you must love Him. And loving Him, you must become like Him. Love begets love. It is a process of induction. Put a piece of iron in the presence of a magnetized body, and the piece of iron for a time becomes magnetized. It is charged with an attractive force in the mere presence of the original force, and as long as you leave the two side by side, they are both magnets alike. Remain side by side with Him who loved us and gave Himself for us, and you too will become a center of power, a permanently attractive force; and like Him you will draw all people unto you, like Him you will be drawn unto all people. That is the inevitable effect of love. Anyone who fulfills that cause must have that effect produced in him or her. Try to give up the idea that religion comes to us by chance, or by mystery, or by caprice. It comes to us by natural law, or by supernatural law, for all law is Divine. Edward Irving went to see a dying boy once, and when he entered the room he just put his hand on the boy's head, and said, "My boy, God loves you," and went away. The boy started from his bed and called out to the people in the house, "God loves me! God loves me!" It changed that boy. The sense that God loved him overpowered him, melted him down, and began creating a new heart in him. That is how the love of God melts down the unlovely hearts in people, and begets in each the new creature who is patient, humble, gentle, and unselfish. And there is no other way to get it. There is no mystery about it. We love others, we love everybody, we love our enemies, because He first loved us.

THE DEFENSE

Now I have a closing sentence or two to add about Paul's reason for singling out love as the supreme possession. It is a remarkable reason. In a single phrase it is this: It lasts. "Love," urges Paul, "never faileth." Then he begins again one of his marvelous lists of the great things of the day, and exposes them one by one. He runs over the things that men thought were going to last, and shows that they are all fleeting and temporary.

"Whether there be prophecies, they shall fail." In those days, every mother hoped her son would become a prophet. For hundreds of years God had not spoken by means of any prophet that was given recognition and authority by the king, as Isaiah and others had been. In those days, the prophet was greater than the king in the eyes of many. Between prophets, men waited wistfully for another messenger to come, and when he finally appeared, hung upon his words as on the very voice of God.

Yet Paul says, "Whether there be prophecies, they shall fail." The Bible is full of prophecies. One by one they have "failed"; that is, having been fulfilled their work is finished; they have nothing more to do now in the world except to feed a devout person's faith.

Then Paul talks about tongues. That was another thing that was greatly coveted. "Whether there be tongues, they shall cease." Many centuries have passed since tongues have been known in this world. They have ceased. Take it in any sense you like. Take it, for illustration merely, as languages in general—a sense that, while not in Paul's mind at all, will point out the general truth. Consider the words in which these chapters were written—Greek. It has gone. Take Latin—the other great tongue of those days. It ceased long ago. Look at the Indian language. It is ceasing. The languages of Wales, of Ireland, and of the Scottish Highlands are dying before our eyes. The most popular book in the English language at the present time, except the Bible, is one of Dickens's works, his *Pickwick Papers*. It is largely written in the language of London street life, and experts assure us that in fifty years it will be unintelligible to the average English reader.

Then Paul goes further, and with even greater boldness adds, "Whether there be knowledge, it shall vanish away." The wisdom of the ancients, where is it? It is wholly gone. You put yesterday's paper in the fire. Its knowledge has vanished away. You buy the old editions of the great encyclopedias for a few dollars. Their knowledge has vanished away. Look how the stagecoach was superseded by the train. Look how electricity has swept hundreds of inventions into oblivion. "Whether there be knowledge, it shall vanish away." At every workshop you will see, in the back-yard, a heap of old iron, a few wheels, a few levers, a few cranks, broken and eaten with rust. Years ago that was the pride of the city. People flocked in from the country to see the great inventions; now they are superseded, their day is done. And all the boasted science and philosophy of this day will soon be old.

At one time at the University of Edinburgh, the greatest figure on the faculty was Sir James Simpson, the discoverer of chloroform. His successor and nephew, Professor Simpson, the story goes, was asked by the librarian of the university to go to the library and pick out books on his subject that were no longer needed. His reply to the librarian was this: "Take every textbook that is more than ten years old, and put it down in the cellar." Sir James Simpson was a great authority and men came from all parts of the earth to consult him. Today, almost the entire teaching of that time is consigned to oblivion. And in every branch of science it is the same. "Now we know in part. We see through a glass darkly."

Can you tell me anything that is going to last? Many things Paul did not condescend to name. He did not mention money, fortune, fame; instead, he

picked out the great things of his time, the things the
best men thought had something in them, and
brushed them peremptorily aside. Paul had nothing
against these things in themselves. All he said about
them was that they would not last. They were great
things, but not supreme things. There were things
beyond them. What we are stretches past what we do,
beyond what we possess. Many things that are
denounced as sins are not sins, but they are temporary. And that is a favorite argument of the New
Testament. John says of the world, not that it is
wrong, but simply that it "passeth away." There is a
great deal in the world that is delightful and beautiful;
there is a great deal in it that is great and engrossing;
but it will not last. All that is in the world—the lust
of the eye, the lust of the flesh, and the pride of life—
lasts only a little while. Therefore, don't love the

world. Nothing that it contains is worth the life and consecration of an immortal soul. The immortal soul must give itself to something that is immortal. And the only immortal things are these: "Now abideth faith, hope, love, but the greatest of these is love."

Some think the time will come when two of these things will also pass away—faith into sight, hope into fruition. Paul does not say so. We know little now about the conditions of the life that is to come. But what is certain is that love must last because God, the eternal God, is love. Covet that everlasting gift, that one thing that is certainly going to stand, that one currency that will be in the universe when all others will be useless and unhonored. You will give yourselves to many things—give yourselves first to love. Hold things in their proportion. *Hold things in their proportion.* Let at least the first great object of our lives be to achieve the character defended in these words, the character—and it is the character of Christ—that is built around love.

I have said this thing is eternal. Did you ever notice how continually John associates love and faith with eternal life? I was not told when I was a boy that "God so loved the world that He gave His only begotten Son, that whosoever believeth in Him should have everlasting life." What I was told, I remember, was that God so loved the world that, if I trusted in Him, I was to have a thing called peace, or I was to have rest, or I was to have joy, or I was to have safety. But I had to find out for myself that whosoever trusteth in Him—that is, whosoever loveth Him, for trust is only the avenue to love—hath everlasting life. The Gospel offers life. Never offer people a thimbleful of Gospel. Do not offer them merely joy, or merely peace, or merely rest, or merely safety; tell them how Christ came to give them a more abundant life than they have, a life abundant in love, and therefore abundant in salvation for themselves and the world. Only then can the Gospel take hold of a person—body, soul, and spirit—and give each part its exercise and reward. Many of the current Gospels are addressed only to a part of human nature. They offer peace, not life; faith, not love; justification, not regeneration. People slip back again from such religion because it has never really held them. Their nature was not all in it. It offered no deeper meaning than that of the life they were living. Surely it stands to reason that only a fuller love can compete with the love of the world.

To love abundantly is to live abundantly, and to love forever is to live forever. Hence, eternal life is inextricably bound with love. We want to live forever

for the same reason that we want to live tomorrow.
Why do you want to live tomorrow? It is because
there is someone who loves you, and whom you want
to see tomorrow, and be with, and love. There is no
other reason why we should live than that we love and
are beloved. It is when a man has no one to love him
that he commits suicide. So long as he has friends,
those who love him and whom he loves, he will live;
because to live is to love. Even the love of a dog will
keep him alive; but let that go and he has no contact
with life, no reason to live. The "energy of life" has
failed. Eternal life also is to know God, and God is
love. This is Christ's own definition. Think about it.
"This is life eternal, that they might know Thee the
only true God, and Jesus Christ whom Thou hast
sent." Love must be eternal. It is what God is. In the
last analysis, then, love is life. Love never faileth, and

life never faileth so long as there is love. That is the philosophy Paul is showing us; the reason why in the nature of things love should be the supreme thing—because it is going to last; because it is an eternal life. That life is a thing that we are living now, not that we get when we die; we will have a poor chance of getting that life when we die unless we are living now. No worse fate can befall a person than to live and grow old alone, unloving and unloved. To be lost is to live in an unregenerate condition, loveless and unloved; and to be saved is to love; and he that dwells in love dwells already in God. For God is love.

Now I have all but finished. How many of you will join me in reading this chapter once a week for the next three months? A man did that once and it changed his whole life. Will you do it? It is for the greatest thing in the world. You might begin by reading it every day, especially the verses that describe the perfect character. "Love suffereth long, and is kind; love envieth not; love vaunteth not itself." Get these ingredients into your life. Then everything that you do is eternal. It is worth doing. It is worth your time. You can't become a saint in your sleep; and to fulfill the conditions required demands a certain amount of prayer and meditation and time, just as improvement in any direction, physical or mental, requires preparation and care. Address yourself to that one thing; at any cost have this transcendent character exchanged for yours. You will find as you look back on your life that the moments that stand out, the moments when you have really lived, are the moments when you have done things in a spirit of love. As you recall the past, above and beyond all transitory pleasures, what you remember are those times when you have done unnoticed things for those around you. I have seen almost all the beautiful things that God has made; I have enjoyed almost every pleasure that He has planned for humankind; and yet as I look back I see standing out four or five experiences when the love of God reflected itself in some poor imitation, some small act of love of mine. Everything else is transitory. Every other good is visionary. But the acts of love that no one knows about, or can ever know about—they never fail.

In the book of Matthew, the Judgment Day is depicted for us in the imagery of One seated on a throne, who divides the sheep from the goats. The test of a person then is not, "How have I believed?" but "How have I loved?" The test of religion, the final test of religion, is not religiousness, but love. I say the final test of religion at that great day is not religiousness, but love; not what I have done, not what I have believed, not what I have achieved, but how I have acted charitably. Sins of commission in that awful indictment are not even referred to. By what we have not done, by sins of omission, we are judged. It could not be otherwise. For the withholding of love is the negation of the Spirit of Christ, the proof that we never knew Him, that for us He lived in vain. It means that He suggested nothing in all our thoughts, that He inspired nothing in all our lives, that we were not once near enough to Him to be seized with the spell of His compassion for the world. It means that:

> "I lived for myself, I thought for myself,
> For myself, and none beside—
> Just as if Jesus had never lived,
> As if He had never died."

THE GREATEST THING IN THE WORLD

It is the Son of Man before whom the nations
of the world will be gathered. It is in the presence of
humanity that we will be charged. And the spectacle
itself, the mere sight of it, will silently judge each
one. There we will meet either those whom we have
met and helped, or the unpitied masses whom we
neglected. No other witness need be summoned. No
charge other than lovelessness will be brought. Be
not deceived. The words that all of us will one day
hear speak not of theology, but of life; not of
churches and saints, but of the hungry and the poor;
not of creeds and doctrines, but of shelter and cloth-
ing; not of Bibles and prayerbooks, but of cups of
cold water in the name of Christ. Thank God the
Christianity of today is coming nearer the world's
needs. Live for that. Thank God people know better
what religion is, what God is, who Christ is, where

Christ is. Who is Christ? He who fed the hungry, clothed the naked, visited the sick. And where is Christ? Where?—whoso shall receive a little child in My name receiveth Me. And who are Christ's? Everyone that loves is born of God.